AMERICA'S UNDISCOVERED

LOVE, TUPELO

ROCKIN' ROAD TRIP

CORVUS
PRESS

www.corvuspress.com

ISBN-13: 978-0-9829239-8-6 (Softcover)

- Published by Corvus Press, Lafayette, LA (Edited by Jeremy Broussard; production and art direction by Angelina Leger)
- Photography by Mary Meghan Mabus, Tupelo, MS
- Cover photo of Bill Cherry by Mary Meghan Mabus
- Cover and internal design by Angelina M. Leger, Lafayette, LA
- Author photo by Nicole Mayeaux, New Orleans, LA
- Printed by Lightning Source

This book is dedicated to my mother, Priscilla Babin,

And, to my Nanny, Jane Anderson

With gratitude.

ACKNOWLEDGEMENTS

The author extends many, many thanks to those who generously supported "Love, Tupleo" through donations on Kickstarter.com, especially: Priscilla Babin, Bernard Bean, Leslie Blanchard, Lisa Brooks, Beverly Easterling, Barb Fuller, Louis C. Marascalco III, Melanie Torbett, and Chole Webre.

TUPELO

All America City!

We Let Our Hospitality Show!

INTRODUCTION

THIS IS NOT A BOOK ABOUT ELVIS PRESLEY. I am not qualified to write such a book, and I certainly don't possess the moxie to pretend any expertise on that extraordinary man's life and work. I admit, though, that I've been skirting the edges of a project like this for a while now; Elvis began making guest appearances in fiction pieces I wrote for college workshop classes about four years ago, and, to my surprise (I was so nervous!), the vignettes in which he showed up were received with delight from some of supportive classmates and grudging admiration from my more critical colleagues. The tried and true bitter whispers that attend most workshop circles evaporated when Elvis made the scene. My fictional Elvis could *do stuff* ... console brokenhearted corporate lawyers, read the minds of unfaithful lovers, and come to the aid of the mathematically challenged. Omnipotent, all-powerful, everlasting Elvis.

I guess I took Elvis on as a totem because he feels like family. My grandmother is a fan – more than a fan, really. She pilgrimages to Memphis each January and August. She is someone I identify with strongly, and I have naturally gravitated toward her interests and tastes. To me, the most fascinating aspect of her personality is her devotion to the artist and her refusal to let his energy and essence leave her life. Her home reflects a level of devotion the likes of which I have never seen elsewhere. The cumulative effect of being surrounded by so many images, so much memorabilia and merchandise and King-themed minutia (refrigerator magnets) is comforting to me. His expression in the posters, prints, and porcelain plates, in the stamps and statues, the books, board games and – you get the picture – is varied. I've seen him joyful, intense, pouty and pious. Elvis every which way. What I'm getting at is that there is a feeling of intense serenity that these images have provided me, a sensation of deep security and family-style safety that transcends his celebrity. Elvis is good people. Elvis is *my* people.

So, the synthesis of scholarship and heritage occurred when I was offered the opportunity to write about the Tupelo Elvis Festival. Say the name of this North Mississippi town in an elevator, a coffee shop, a boardroom, an ashram. Go ahead. Turn to the person next to you and say, "Tupelo, Mississippi." Twenty bucks says you'll get a simple reply: "Elvis Presley." Although Memphis is known as a de facto mecca for fans continental and international alike, a quick survey of the Elvis fans in my life was all I needed to identify Mississippi's edge: the Birthplace. I capitalize it here because in some circles, it is spoken that way, with reverence. More on that in a little while.

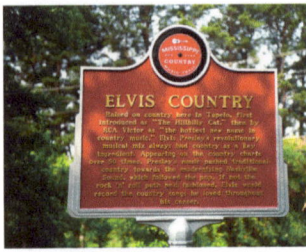

I gave myself about thirty seconds to mull over the offer to create this book, then got to work pounding keys. Google coughed up the festival's website, and I got a little word of mouth through a phone call to the friend of a friend who had attended the festival in its earliest days. Let's call him S. S. let me know that the original aim of the festival was to feature acts that claimed Elvis as a creative influence, as well as some of the musicians who'd performed with EP back in the day. Acts like Jerry Lee Lewis, Charlie Daniels Band, Marty Stuart, and the Jordanaires entertained the festival's first audiences on the site of the town's fairgrounds, hallowed turf that had seen hometown shows in '56, just before the Elvis explosion commenced proper. S. supported my interest in the festival, with one caveat:

"That festival's not exactly what it used to be..." He meant that big names had been replaced with local acts and country bands. He said it gently, though, and wished me well in my exploration of North Mississippi's jewel; snugly situated in a geographic region he called "the tail end of Appalachia."

I needed to get with the "powers that be." I called the number connected to the name on the website, one Debbie Brangenburg. That phone call was my introduction to what I now know as hospitality, Tupelo style. I expected at least a guarded, "Now, who are you with?" Nope. We set a date to meet two weeks later at her office directly off Tupelo's Main Street.

Debbie is the backbone of the city of Tupelo's determined crusade to keep the place pristine. She spends her nine-to-fives helming Tupelo's Downtown Main Street Association, aiming her energy at preserving the wonder and restoring the worn. A great deal of her professional time is focused specifically on the Tupelo Elvis Festival; she supposes about fifty percent. The day we met, she put the whirlwind treatment on my head: the Elvis Festival is *complex*. It has to be, in order for it to go off hitch-less, for people to just make the scene and enjoy. We spent a good while talking business that day, and I got the feeling that Debbie had a deeper connection to making the first weekend of every June something special. I hinted around at my assumption, and she gave me the most marvelous story in return: Debbie had an Elvis grandma, too.

Her name was Archie Dean McAlilly (Grandma Archie Dean), and she taught Debbie how to dance. Over her bed, four pictures were displayed: a picture of Archie Dean, and one of her sister. A picture of Debbie's father and a picture of Elvis Presley. Debbie Brangenburg was born to lead this festival.

The simple festival breakdown is this: a long weekend packed with what one would expect - the kinds of things that make every festival fun: carnival rides, a parade, local bands (the ones S. told me about), festival food, a ton of Elvis stuff to buy, shuttles to the Birthplace, a re-enactment of the purchase of ten-year-old EP's first guitar, and an Elvis Tribute Artist Contest. Cue the screeching brakes.

It works this way: forget Vegas wedding chapels. Erase that image from your mind, please. And yes, I had to leave a bit of doubt at the door, as well. I learned that what I would be experiencing at the Tupelo Elvis Festival is far removed from karaoke shtick - the operative word is competition. The stakes are pretty high, too. Yes, there is a cash prize, as well as a brand-new guitar from Tupelo Hardware to win, and a trophy; more meaningful, though, is the opportunity that winning the Ultimate Elvis Tribute Artist contest in Tupelo earns one lucky guy: the chance to compete in the Ultimate contest in Memphis. In August. During Elvis Week. Winning Tupelo and Memphis is career-making; winning both the same year is monumental. I'll introduce you to the man who can claim those honors a few pages down the road.

Leaving Tupelo after that first visit, I felt like I was rocketing out of the past via the Natchez Trace. My mind was churning the memories of all the people and places I had encountered in those three days, parsing out ways to fit everything into a single document. Debbie had, and has continued to, connect me to the folks who keep the heart of Tupelo rocking and rolling. I owe her a tremendous debt of gratitude for that. I returned to Tupelo several times more in the spring and summer of 2011, layering impressions and collecting experiences. The visits culminated in the Elvis Festival, the ostensible reason for the existence of this book.

June rolled around and I thought I had a pretty good idea about what to expect. By that time, I'd watched countless hours of video footage of Elvis and as many of the Tribute Artists slated to perform that I could find, connected with the people who make Tupelo extraordinary, eaten plenty of Mississippi comfort food, walked down Tupelo's Main Street many times, and talked to a bunch of strangers who treated me like a friend *instantly*. I'd gotten all misty-eyed in the Birthplace, and stood in front of the Lyric Theatre with my mouth wide open; I assumed that I was ready.

Back on the Trace on my way to the Festival, I reflected on the conversations I'd had at the beginning of my adventure. The one with S. about the ways in which the festival was "not like it used to be." Echoing in my mind was Debbie's answer to that assertion - the Festival had changed because of the fans. The fans let Debbie know that what they really wanted was the experience of watching Elvis perform live. Yes, this is something that can never be, but not for some folks' lack of effort. The expression "keeper of the flame" comes to mind. Let me show you what I mean...

HOMETOWN

NATCHEZ TRACE

I live in South Louisiana. Each time I road-tripped to Tupelo, I took a route that eventually blended into the Natchez Trace Parkway. If this option is available to you, *go there*. The Trace is roughly four hundred miles of the most hypnotic highway I have ever set wheels on. The molasses pace (50 mph) of a back-in-time two lane with nothing to see except wall-to-wall gorgeous green will set your mind on Tupelo time. It is what the Trace is missing – billboards (or advertising of any kind), fast food, gas stations – that make the ride so rich. The silence of those woods is eerie in the most enchanting sense of the word, and campsites and trails for hiking and biking are tucked invitingly throughout. In other words, an ideal off switch for the reality burdened.

LYRIC THEATRE

#2
MAP
PG 58

No venue in Tupelo is more fitting to host the Elvis Festival than the Lyric, and the joint is jumpin' come festival time. The tribute artist contest happens here, as well as packed evening concerts featuring past winners, along with appearances by some of EP's inner circle. I had the opportunity to see Sonny Burgess and the Pacers with DJ Fontana perform on the festival's opening night, and Fontana performed again with 2008 tribute artist winner Victor Trevino, Jr. at his feature show. Monumental night.

Ninety nine years of performing arts history, along with some crucial Elvis mythology have gone down on the Lyric's stage, as well as in the seats – the balcony, specifically.

Rumor has it that the balcony was the scene of Elvis' first kiss, back in the days of the Lyric's run as a movie theatre. An iconic anchor of downtown Tupelo with its vintage façade and flashing marquis, the Lyric is an easy walk from Main Street. Tribute artists have the honor of pacing the boards their hero set ablaze way back when, and for members of the audience, the view is excellent – there are no "cheap seats" here, and taking in a show in the cool darkness is a welcome respite from the early summer swelter. The vintage setting completes the story framed onstage, and I recommend that you catch a production by Tupelo Community Theatre when you pay a visit to Tupelo – the Lyric is its official home.

MAIN STREET VINTAGE GUITARS

I got the word on the brothers Gillantine, owners of Main Street Vintage Guitars, from an acquaintance, a Delta girl transplanted to my neck of the swamp who readily told me that some of the most interesting Mississippians she knows are from Tupelo. She was talking about Mike Gillantine specifically, and visiting the haven of guitar resurrection he runs with his brother Matt made me a believer. Pay attention to the name: vintage guitars only. Seventy gorgeous ones, ready for sale, line the walls of the carefully renovated space that has occupied a corner of Tupelo's Main Street for over one hundred years. Matt was making music and engineering records at Oxford's Sweet Tea studios when he got the call from his brother about a building for sale and a business to start in Tupelo. Ready for a change, he headed home. Mike's a luthier, meaning he can build guitars from scratch, as well as painstakingly restore ones that are damaged or antique. His second floor workshop is an expanse of raw, light-filled loft where he labors over the wounded guitars of the likes of Jack White, Elvis Costello, members of the band Modest Mouse, and childhood guitar hero Johnny Marr of the Smiths. Unexpected? Not in a place like Tupelo. These native sons' artistry bolsters Tupelo's promise to keep the music alive.

4
MAP
PG 58

TUPELO HARDWARE

What did you want for your tenth birthday? Elvis wanted a rifle. His mama, Gladys, had other ideas – she wanted her boy to have a guitar. Mother and son visited Tupelo Hardware that January day in 1945 to buy an eight dollar (roughly) birthday gift, and left with history in their hands. Imagine a world in which the rifle had won out ... impossible.

Tupelo Hardware is ... a hardware store. Yes, a real business with the kinds of things you would expect to find in any hardware store, in any town. Need nuts, bolts, screws, a can of spray paint? A pocket knife or a cast-iron griddle? All available at Tupelo Hardware – the place is packed with dry goods. Souvenirs, too: t-shirts, and key chains, guitar picks, and ... guitars. You can buy your own self a guitar at Tupelo Hardware. Most days, the store gets its fair share of visitors who want to see the exact spot where Elvis first held a guitar. Tours are available daily, and a letter from Mr. Forrest L. Bobo, the man who made the sale that birthday, is displayed on the beautifully maintained, high wooden counter, detailing the exact events that led to the monumental purchase. Don't miss this stop on your Tupelo tour, it is essential.

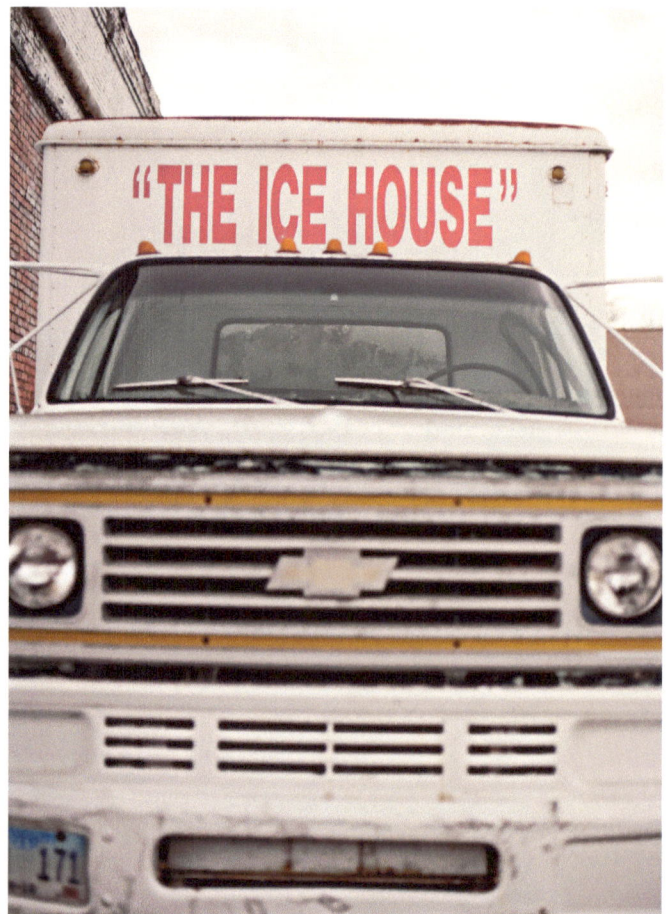

GARDNER-WATSON ICEHOUSE/THE SILVERMOON CLUB

6 MAP PG 58

Picture it: my first day in Tupelo. I drop my bags, grab a snack, and jump back in the car for a twilight ride around town. I asked for a simple, singular direction at my hotel's front desk: "Which way to Main Street?"

Discovery mission number one was a huge success - the next day I met with Debbie to get the local word on what to see and who to know. I remembered something special I had seen the night before as we wrapped up our visit.

"Hey...what's that brick building over there," I hiked a thumb over my shoulder in the direction of the next block, "the one with the big mural on the side?"

Allow me to explain. The Gardner-Watson Icehouse is located a few blocks back from Main Street, in what was once a Ford dealership. A native of Newport Arkansas, Charlie Watson moved to Tupelo in 1961 when he married Peggy Gardner. His roots in entertainment run deep; he owned the thousand-seat Silver Moon Club in Newport before relocating in Tupelo, and the Icehouse pays tribute to that time in foot-high letters that overlook a polk salad garden near the club's door. The Icehouse became what it is today in 1999, the Elvis Festival's inaugural year, and what it is today is a cultural vault of sorts, a place where all kinds of festival revelry happens.

Debbie explained to me that Charlie has an awesome Elvis collection. I knew what she meant instantly. Memorabilia, pictures, *stuff.* Authentic, special stuff in this case. The Icehouse is a private club, though – I'd need an introduction to see the treasures inside.

Fast forward to my next Tupelo trip, same song second verse: I'm driving around downtown. This time, I notice something's different about the Icehouse. Cars in the parking lot.. The door's open, lights are on inside. I took a chance and stepped into Elvis Wonderland.

I got a traditional Tupelo welcome from Charlie Watson that afternoon, which is to say that, when I announced the reason for my visit, he invited me in and gave me a world-class tour of the wall-to-wall photographs, posters, and paintings that cover most available surfaces. Each has a story, and Charlie knows them all. He invited me to visit again at festival time, when the Icehouse is filled with visitors, volunteers, and tribute artists mingling, eating the delish home cooked buffet the Watsons provide, and enjoying impromptu musical performances by any musician who wants to take the stage. In the center of all this activity are Charlie and Peggy Watson, two of the most gracious and generous people I met while researching this project. They are one of the reasons I love Tupelo.

7
MAP
PG 58

JOHNNIE'S DRIVE IN

The burgers are not exactly like Mama made, but EP loved 'em and it looks like they're here to stay. This drive-in/eat-in hasn't changed much, a move that could be filed under "it ain't broke." Actually, the opposite is true – Johnnie's enjoys a brisk business from locals who grew up on their burgers and bar-b-que, as well as those visiting town to TCB; Johnnie's is a quick ride around the corner from the Birthplace, and a must for those who want the complete Tupelo experience.

MISSISSIPPI
COUNTRY
MUSIC TRAIL

ELVIS COUNTRY

Raised on country here in Tupelo, first introduced as "The Hillbilly Cat," then by RCA Victor as "the hottest new name in country music," Elvis Presley's revolutionary musical mix always had country as a key ingredient. Appearing on the country charts over 50 times, Presley's music pushed traditional country towards the modernizing Nashville Sound, which followed the pop, if not the rock 'n' roll path he'd fashioned. Elvis would record the country songs he loved throughout his career.

BIRTHPLACE

If you ever find yourself in Tupelo and you have time to do just one thing, promise me something, please? Promise me you will visit Elvis Presley's Birthplace. About 80,000 people put it on their list each year, and a great number of them are visiting from other countries – the majority of those international visitors are from the United Kingdom (I heard British accents *every single time* I visited). Yes, this tiny white house is a national treasure.

Simple to find, too. Boogie all the way down Main into East Tupelo, just over the train tracks. Pass Johnnie's on the right, or better yet, grab some lunch before you go. Signs will direct you to ... a neighborhood. For some reason, I was surprised to find that the Birthplace exists among regular homes where people are living their regular lives. I guess I was expecting the place to be surrounded by golden light atop a bluff, or underneath an "Eat at Joes!"-style blinking neon sign. That's a Memphis way of thinking, I've learned.

I return over and over to a simple description I jotted down the day I drove on to the grounds of the birthplace for the first time. The place is earthy. Warm, natural, green, sumptuously verdant. Surprised? I was, too, at first, but I learned that this simple setting is a reflection of the Elvis that Tupelo cherishes so deeply – the young boy who probably played in the woods facing the house; the boy who discovered a love of music in the Assembly of God church that has been moved onto the grounds, the boy who was born (along with his twin brother, Jesse Garon) in the front room of a house that measures something like fifteen by thirty feet. Pace those dimensions out in your home, and imagine that it is the sum total of your living space. Cozy, right?

Thing is, the home is cozy, and very inviting. It has a sweetly antique aroma, like syrup and dust, and I admit that a big old sentimental lump forms in my throat each time I step over the threshold. The furnishing is extremely simple, replicas of the original – the Presleys sold most everything they owned when they left Tupelo for Memphis in 1948. The front room served as the Presley's parlor and bedroom, and a fireplace topped with a family portrait occupies the wall that divides the space in half. At that midline, a doorway leads to the home's other room, a modest kitchen. There's a back door on the far wall, and that is it. The surroundings are less impactful than the feeling the Birthplace holds, though – something like a semi-sacred weight that represents the imprinted emotions of the people who have walked its floors these last forty years, I guess. That's my take on it.

> *The Birthplace on the whole, though, has such an air of reverence, and a connection to the natural surroundings it occupies ...*

Over a gentle rise on the grounds stands the Assembly of God church I mentioned earlier. The building was moved from its original site nearby and restored inside and out. It has a special significance on account of the fact that Elvis first learned to love music there, and it is the first place he sang in public. Near the church is a modern chapel and a small museum with some of EP's personal stuff (belt buckles! A menorah!); as well as a gift shop, of course. The Birthplace on the whole, though, has such an air of reverence, and a connection to the natural surroundings it occupies, that the whole "tourist" story seems like a major disconnect. When I think of it now, writing this, I remember it as a place of heavy stillness and a simple kind of peace.

ELVIS PRESLEY AND THE BLUES

Elvis Presley revolutionized popular music by blending the blues he first heard as a youth in Tupelo with country, pop, and gospel. Many of the first songs Elvis recorded for the Sun label in Memphis were covers of earlier blues recordings by African Americans, and he continued to incorporate blues into his records and live performances for the remainder of his career.

TRIBUTE

TUPELO ELVIS PRESLEY FAN CLUB

TUPELO'S ELVIS PRESLEY FAN CLUB BEGAN ALONGSIDE AN IRONING BOARD. Sixteen year old Barbara Mallory was doing chores one day in 1956 when a song came on the radio that she says stopped her cold. The song was "Blue Moon of Kentucky." The artist: a boy near her age who grew up just down the road, Elvis Presley. Barbara rallied a few of her cousins and friends, and the "Elvis Presley Sweethearts" was born. The girls made as many local shows as they could, including the 1956 homecoming show at Fairpark. They reckoned that starting a fan club would help attract their hero's attention.

Barbara brought her Sweetheart scrapbook to our meeting in Tupelo, and led me through the fragile pages, lingering over especially meaningful clippings and notes. She gave me the Sweetheart's photo, too – she's the one holding the scrapbook in it. We visited for a good while that day; her continued devotion to the music is evident. She recollected the five Elvis concerts she attended over the years, and we talked about the songs of his she loves the most, ballads like "Help Me Make it Through the Night," and gospel. The responsibilities of family life shut down the Sweethearts after a few years, and the city of Tupelo revived the club in 2006, in commemoration of Elvis' homecoming show at Fairpark.

The club's current incarnation has about 700 members worldwide, and hey, you can join, too – the twenty-dollar due date is January 8th of each year, naturally.

Member dues work hard. The club is an Elvis Festival sponsor and a $5,000 scholarship is awarded each year to a deserving high school senior. The club supplements the fund with sales of their cookbook and the proceeds from their Birthplace license tag. You gotta move to Mississippi to get one of those. Lay eyes on it and you might want to.

Barbara Mallory is still an active fan club member, and a festival fixture. I had assumed that, as the club's founder, she still held the title of club President as well, but she passed those duties on a few years ago, for another role: "They named me First Lady, I think."

> " *They named me First Lady, I think.* "

SUPERFANS

I really wanted to meet some seriously devoted fans at the festival, and asking around paid off for me, big time. Festival organizers connected me with Mary Pat Van Epps of Memphis, and I shadowed her like gravy on rice for the entire festival weekend. I would be utterly remiss if I did not mention the close-knit group of fellow fans she rolls with: her friends Lydia and Gina (hometown: Baton Rouge, Louisiana), and Mary Pat's sister, Libby, who also hails from Memphis. The ladies were front row center for every concert, every performance, and they were regular visitors to Charlie Watson's icehouse, as well. I admired their energy; come eleven o'clock each night, when I was dragging, they were still going strong. We sat down for a good long talk on the last morning of the festival, and I asked them to tell me what they love most about Tupelo, what the place means to them as fans. They gave me some gems, to be sure.

All agreed that Tupelo has a special place in their hearts because, as Lydia put it, "the essence of Elvis started on that street," meaning at the Birthplace. The character and compassion that Elvis possessed, they believe, was a direct result of his formative years in Tupelo, surrounded by his extended family and church community. The acceptance they have found at the festival in Tupelo is another draw; being among the people who, "if you are enjoying a song, or in a moment, nobody thinks: freak!" Visiting Tupelo, and spending time among "our people," they said, and enjoying Elvis music is restorative, good for the soul.

The ladies shared their individual "a ha!" moments regarding their devotion to EP, and sadly, those moments occurred after August of 1977, which makes sense, in a way - each was busy with work and family in the years that Elvis was touring regularly, so his music was something that they enjoyed, but at a distance. Mary Pat described a pivotal visit to Graceland during Elvis week, and her discovery that "Elvis has a song for every emotion," an assertion that I agree with, now that I have spent some significant time with his songs and films. Libby, upon moving back to Memphis after some time spent away from home is the only member of the group to have seen Elvis perform live – the show was in New York City. She remembers, though, that she "kept thinking that I was going to meet him and marry him." Lydia remembered visiting Graceland for the 25 year anniversary of Elvis' death, and experiencing a revelation when she "saw all the checks and awards in the trophy room" (Elvis was known as spectacularly generous to friends and strangers alike), "and I saw what a truly good person he was ... I fell in love with a dead man."

Honestly, what else is there to say? Mary Pat put fandom into succinct perspective for me when she paraphrased Elvis' long-time friend George Klein: "If you're an Elvis Presley fan, no explanation is necessary; if you're not, no explanation is possible."

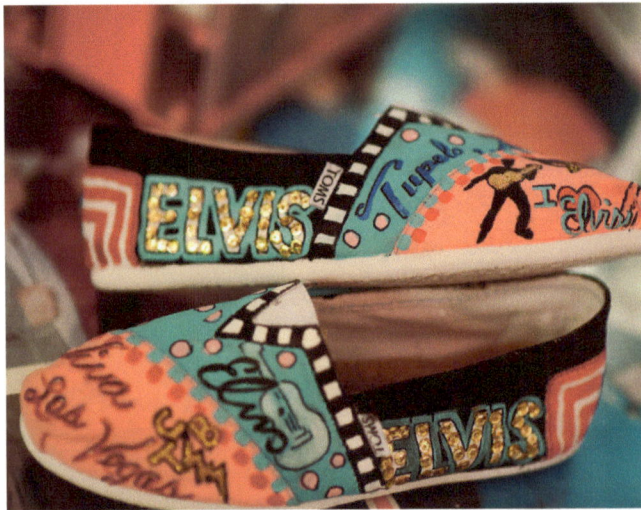

MERCH

Lord, they got Elvis stuff at the festival, and people love to buy it. The usual suspects: license plates, bumper stickers, t-shirts, coffee mugs. A few surprises: lip balm, tooth brushes, purses, and temporary tattoos (those are cool). What would a festival be without a little somethin' to take home with you, besides that sunburn? I get the feeling that these items carry a deeper significance for those who collect them, that they are more than just plastic remembrances of a weekend in their lives. They are more like talismans, totems ... charms. Forgive me for getting all metaphysical about it, but in a way I think that every pilgrim needs a relic from the holy land, and these fit the bill just fine.

THE POSTER

File this under: merchandise, subcategory: brilliant. This image sealed the deal for me. My first trip to Tupelo was a fact-finding mission of sorts; let's say I was 99 percent sold on making this book. Then I saw Tupelo native Lucia Randle's poster. Y'all … I got *excited*. I had to meet this artist! So I did – barged into her office at Reed's Department store on Main Street, where Lucia spends her days as Director of Marketing for Mississippi's oldest – 105 years – family owned department store (her boss is Tupelo mayor, Jack Reed). Lucia could not have been more gracious in explaining her creative process to me, which included collaging the "Laughing Elvis" image with hand-colored letters culled from pages of a prayer missal and the frayed edge of a scrap from a sketchbook. The colors were chosen for their warmth and vitality, and though she fretted over the outcome, wanting to please, she needn't have … the picture's pure magic; she's designed the 2012 Tupelo Elvis Festival poster, too.

"Before Elvis there was nothing."
John Lennon

2012
elvis festival
may 31 - june 3 • tupelo, mississippi

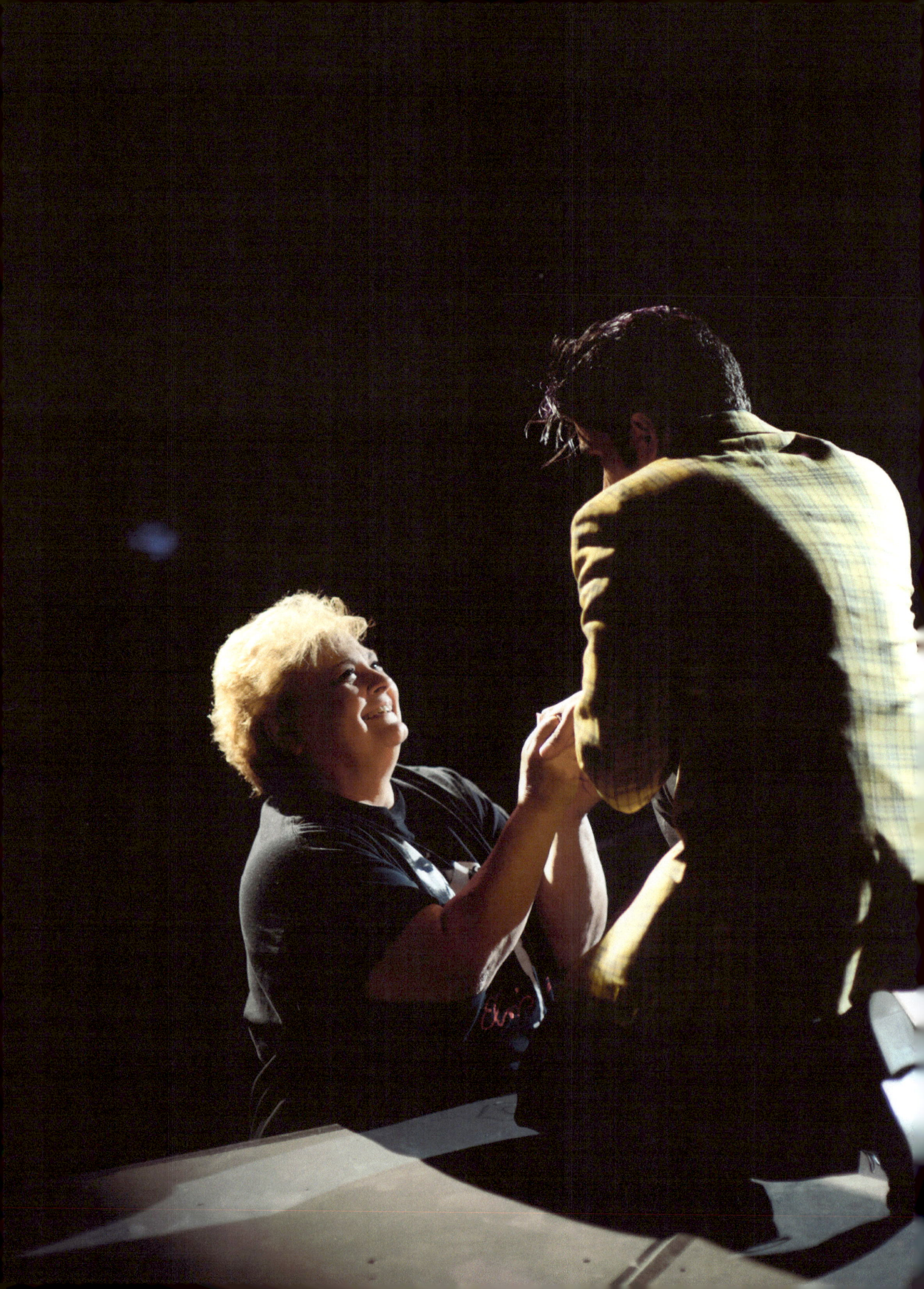

THE 'I' WORD

In order to attempt to accurately describe what a tribute artist is, what a tribute artist does, and what one is about, I feel compelled to detail what a tribute artist is not – or at least what an authentic one shouldn't be. I've had the opportunity to ask friends and strangers their impression of a person who would aspire to pay tribute to Elvis Presley by dressing similarly and performing his songs, and the great majority immediately blurted out a word which now makes me cringe: impersonator. Yes, Elvis Presley impersonators do exist. The folks in charge of Hollywood would have us believe that they are as plentiful as ant hills in an overgrown pasture, but those dime-a-dozen caricatures are as bland as a pan of unseasoned white gravy. An impersonator capitalizes on worn out, inaccurate stereotypes; I won't bore you with the details. A tribute artist is dedicated to the art of transportation, plain and simple. The purpose of each performance is to invite the audience to drop the story of reality and spend some time experiencing ... Elvis. Full-on suspension of disbelief happens when a skilled tribute artist takes over, and the very best ones disappear to themselves when the music begins. Their audiences are lost, as well, in memories, in imagination.

BRANDON BENNETT

Brandon won Tupelo in 2007, then Memphis in 2008. Now, the Ponchatoula, Louisiana native tributes full time. Growing up, his mom was the devoted EP fan, and when people began noticing his uncanny resemblance to the man, he merged his love of vocal performance (he got his start in the church choir – sound familiar?) with total immersion in the Elvis catalog. "If I was listening to music, it was Elvis Presley."

VICTOR TREVINO, JR.

Tupelo's 2008 winner favors Tupelo for its genuine hospitality, but he notes that performing there carries some added pressure - expectations of an authentic take on the 50's tunes he performs are especially high for festival fans. The early career-era hits seem fitting for the 26 year old Fort Worth native - he appreciates the period because of the risky, barrier-busting musical choices Elvis made, choices that "pushed the doors down for other musicians."

BILL CHERRY

Bill captured the title in Tupelo, and then the Ultimate in Memphis in 2009 – dream come true stuff , to be sure, but he wanted me to know upfront. "none of us are Elvis and none of us will ever be." Obvious, I know, but it echoed the sentiment I heard from so many of the guys I interviewed at the festival. Like Bill, they aimed "to put on a tribute that is respectful."

Bill's dad, a Pentecostal minister, nurtured his early love of gospel and rock and roll; he was Bill's first stage crew, in a way. When Bill was a kid, his dad would throw an Elvis record on the turntable and work the flashlight strobe while Bill sang for the family. Elvis movies showed him a lifestyle that he thought looked pretty appealing. Bill plans to perform for as long as he can keep it authentic. "I'm just a keeper of the flame…but let's not forget the flame."

KEVIN MILLS

Kevin first visited Tupelo at age 11, a visit that formed his childhood dream: to become a tribute artist. He told me that "winning Tupelo is an honor and a privilege; I think it has the spirit of Elvis." That spirit informs Kevin's work deeply – he began focusing on the gospel songs EP loved, songs that reflected his Tupelo roots, in 2010.

Important to Kevin, too, is his connection with Elvis fans. He oversees every aspect of his career without the help of a manager, handling everything from booking gigs and marketing to personally answering each letter and phone call from the fans who attend his shows. With a solid annual appearance schedule, he stresses the crucial support of his family, who travels with him for summer concerts. Why does he do it? "You have to love your art, and take care of yourself, too."

CODY SLAUGHTER

Just 20 years old (he turned 20 at the festival) this Harrison, Arkansas native has logged as much time as a tribute artist as some of his colleagues twice his age. An Elvis fan since age six, Cody works full time as a tribute artist, and won the Elvis Festival's competition in 2011. An extremely affable young guy, winning left him utterly speechless ... almost. A few stunned seconds after the announcement was made, Cody took the microphone and thanked "my best friend, the reason for everything. That's Elvis."

JAY DUPUIS

Two years ago, Jay Dupuis was installing alarm systems for a living. He currently performs as Elvis twelve times a week. Talk about an accelerated path to tribute. Jay credits the mentorship of Brandon Bennett with helping him to develop his look and act. He's got a fantastic singing voice, too, and watching him perform was kind of a revelation for me – I'd heard that his "Polk Salad Annie" was a home run, and that is no lie. Jay's tribute confirms the notion that some songs are truly revitalized onstage.

JASON BAGLIO

Jason's career trajectory is a testament to persistence and devotion. The 2011 Elvis Festival was his third shot at competing in Tupelo, a place he has a strong affection for because "this is where the legend was born." Jason supports the idea that festival fans are Elvis fans first, and that if he can recreate the EP feeling on a small scale, he feels successful. He believes in emulating the spirit of Elvis in "how we treat people" is the ultimate tribute, and has massive respect for his fellow tribute artists. "It's all about Elvis, not about us."

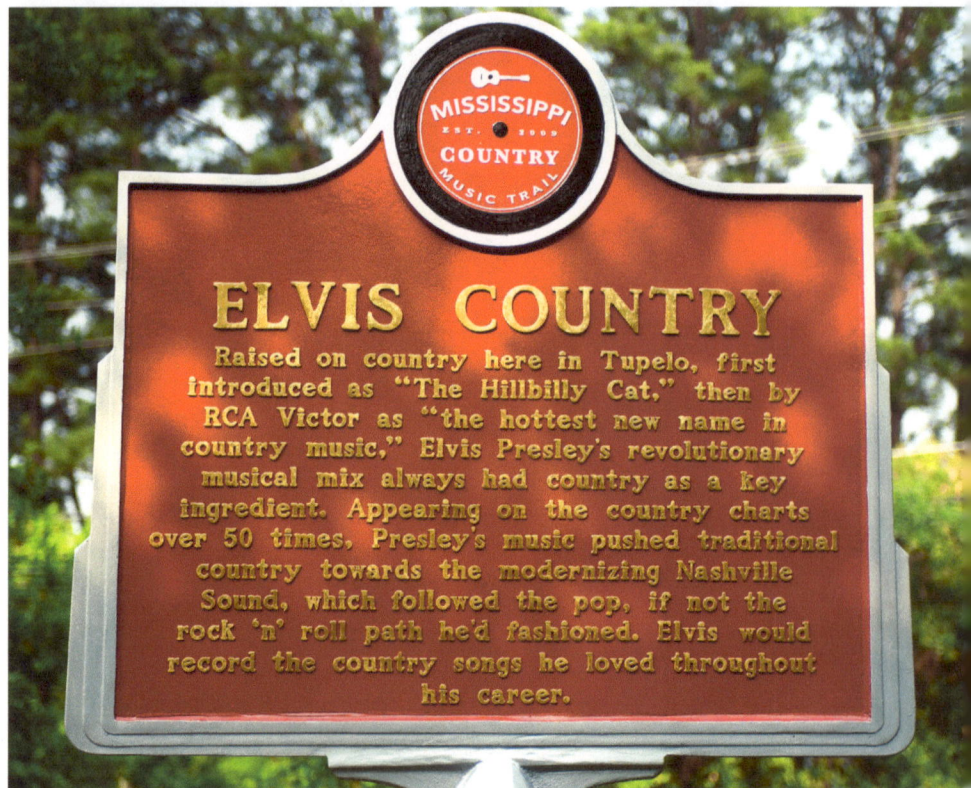

ELVIS COUNTRY

Raised on country here in Tupelo, first introduced as "The Hillbilly Cat," then by RCA Victor as "the hottest new name in country music," Elvis Presley's revolutionary musical mix always had country as a key ingredient. Appearing on the country charts over 50 times, Presley's music pushed traditional country towards the modernizing Nashville Sound, which followed the pop, if not the rock 'n' roll path he'd fashioned. Elvis would record the country songs he loved throughout his career.

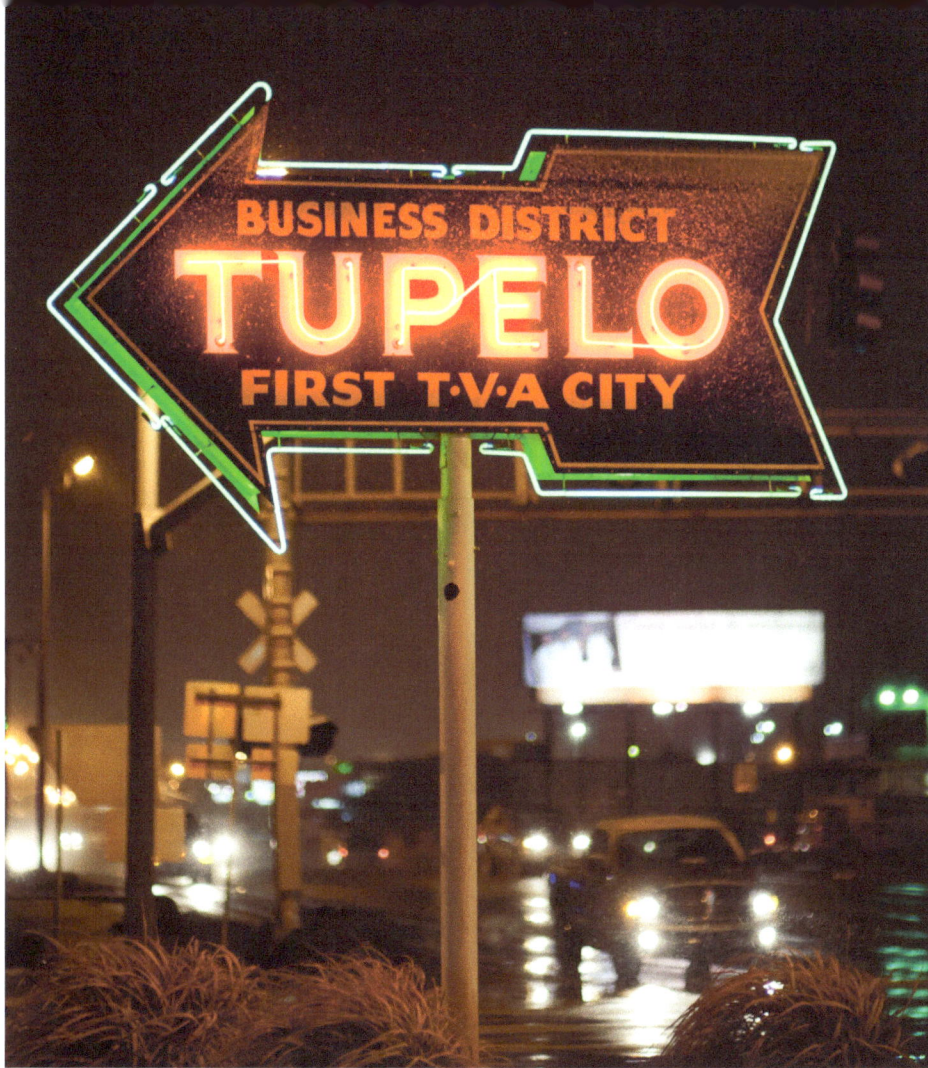

LOVE, TUPELO

We've reached the end of our road together, y'all. Thanks for coming along. I hope that in reading this book – this record of a time and a place-in-time, you have felt the desire to experience the magic of Tupelo for yourself. I know, "magic" is a little bit flimsy here, and that I've left myself wide open to be dismissed as an idealist, or an escapist, or some other kind of ... –ist, but magic is what I have experienced there.

To know Tupelo is to love the place. I consider the town's singular combination of sweetness and soul a kind of valentine to the world, hence this book's title. Yes, love is a strong and risky word, up for interpretation, and fraught with the influence of personal experience. But, if you believe in the at-first-sight variety of love, chances are good that a sojourn to North Mississippi is in order.

Yes, visit Tupelo the first week in June, and take in the Elvis Festival. Even if you only like Elvis music a little bit; even if you think that Memphis or Vegas is what Elvis is all about. If you ask me, the perfect Tupelo day includes a bit of everything I've shown you here – but do yourself a favor: stay awhile, you won't be disappointed. I promise, you will love Tupelo.

TUPELO, MS

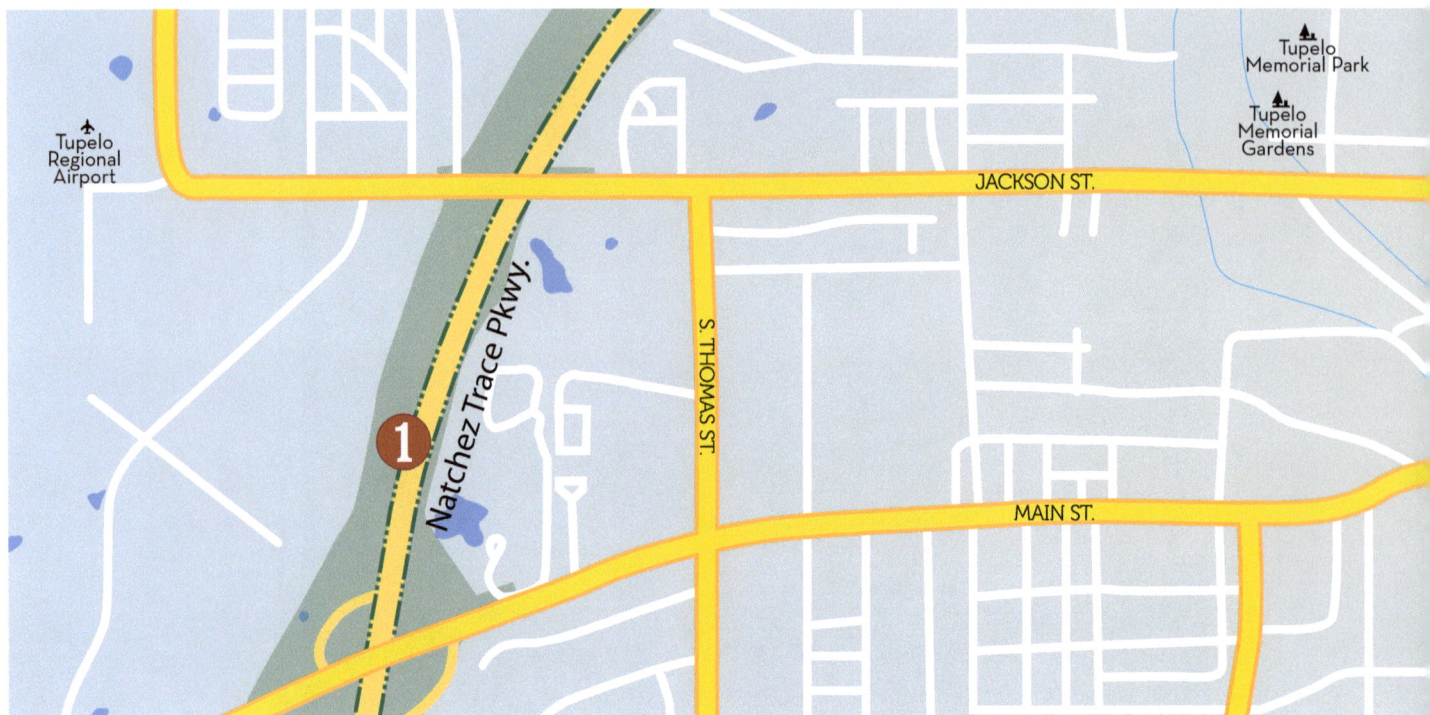

1 NATCHEZ TRACE PARKWAY

2 LYRIC THEATRE
201 North Broadway St.
(662) 844-1935

3 MAIN STREET VINTAGE GUITARS
130 W Main St.
(662) 842-9697
www.pwogs.com

4 TUPELO HARDWARE COMPANY, INC.
114 W. Main St.
(662) 842-4637

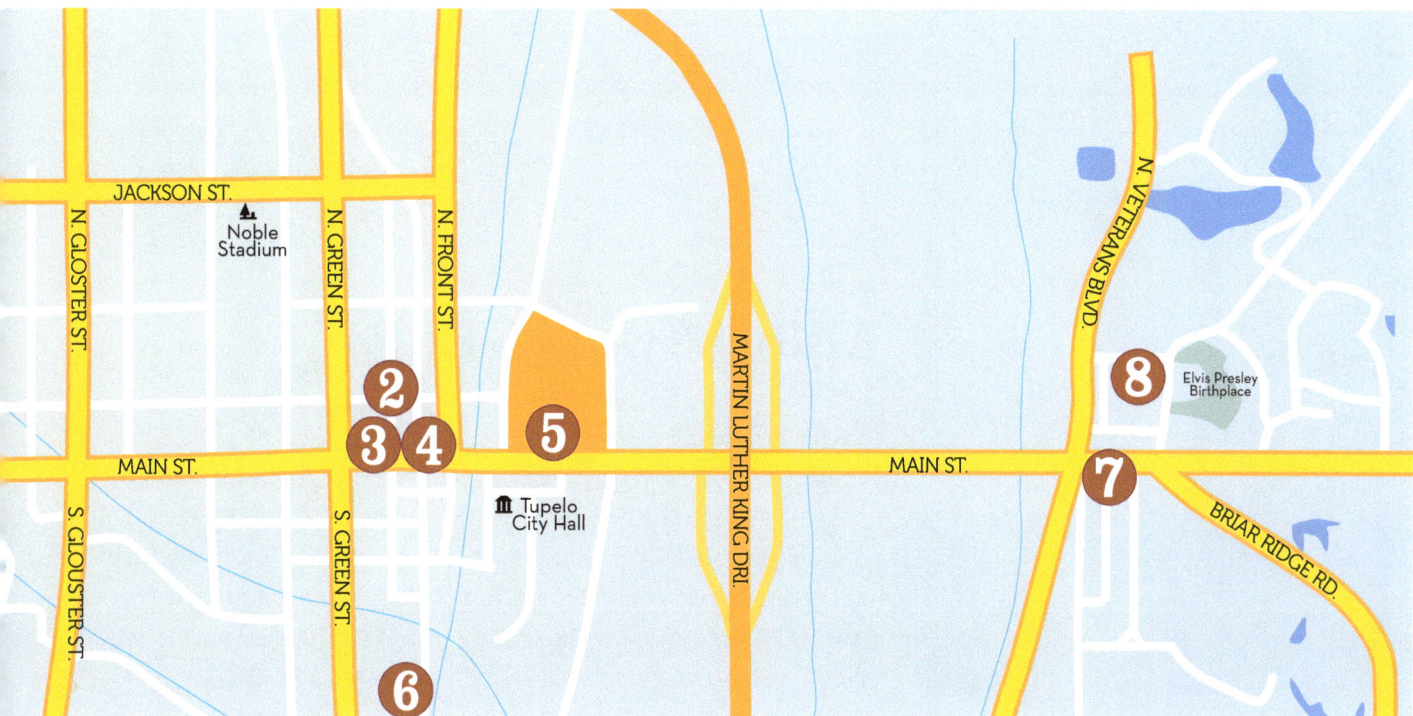

5 FAIRPARK PARK

6 GARDNER-WATSON ICEHOUSE/
THE SILVER MOON CLUB

Corner of Broadway St. and Spring St.

7 JOHNNIE'S DRIVE IN

908 E Main St.

(662) 842-6748

8 ELVIS PRESLEY BIRTHPLACE
AND MUSEUM

306 Elvis Presley Dr.

(662) 841-1245

www.elvispresleybirthplace.com

ABOUT THE AUTHOR

JANE V. BLUNSCHI is a writer and student living in Lafayette, Louisiana. Her creative influences include roots music, magic realism fiction, the paintings of Frida Kahlo and specialty meats. The aim of her work is to reveal the glorious eccentricities of the South, produce exquisitely humorous fiction and write colorfully ever after. Jane credits the effects of growing up "Steel Magnolias" in north Louisiana for her unique worldview and relentless search for her relationship to "belle."

ABOUT THE PHOTOGRAPHER

MARY MEGHAN MABUS is a full time photographer in Tupelo, Mississippi. She enjoys photographing different genres: babies, children, live entertainment, weddings and portraits.

The perks of her job include: travelling to picturesque locations such as Belize, Cancun, Cape Cod, and Chicago to photograph weddings, an all access pass to the Elvis Tribute Artist competition at the Tupelo Elvis Festival and meeting dozens of Elvi every year.

She would be content if every day included cool fall weather, reading in a hammock, good music and a nap.

She likes to tent camp anywhere from the Grand Canyon to the Florida coast with her husband, Josh and a group of friends. She has three step-children and an adorable dog, Elsa; she loves to bake, and is active in her church, Origins.

She is an expert wedding cake taster.

BACK COVER PHOTOS (L to R): Johnnie's Drive In, Lyric Theatre and Tupelo Welcome Sign.
BOTTOM LEFT CORNER: Bill Cherry performing in Lyric Theatre for Tupelo Elvis Festival.
Photos by Mary Meghan Mabus. To see more photos of Tupelo by Mary Meghan, visit www.mwptupelo.com.

CORVUS PRESS HIDDEN TRAVELS™

WANT MORE BOOKS LIKE THIS? The Hidden Travels series of books focuses on day trips to places less traveled and hidden finds usually reserved for locals. Why be a tourist when you can be a Hidden Traveler? Discover the hidden world around you at www.HiddenTravels.com.

LIVE LOVE LOCAL

Proceeds from the sale of each copy of "Love, Tupelo" are donated to the **Downtown Tupelo Mainstreet Association**. For more information, visit http://tupelomainstreet.com.

For more information on the **Tupelo Elvis Festival**, vist http://tupeloelvisfestival.com.

CORVUS PRESS

www.CorvusPress.com

www.ingramcontent.com/pod-product-compliance
Lightning Source LLC
Chambersburg PA
CBHW042006080426

42733CB00003B/28